A Note to Parents an

DK READERS is a compelling new reading programme for children, designed in conjunction with leading literacy experts, including Cliff Moon M.Ed., Honorary Fellow of the University of Reading. Cliff Moon has spent many years as a teacher and teacher educator specializing in reading and has written more than than 140 books for children and teachers. He reviews regularly for teachers' journals.

Beautiful illustrations and superb full-colour photographs combine with engaging, easy-to-read stories to offer a fresh approach to each subject in the series. Each DK READER is guaranteed to capture a child's interest while developing his or her reading skills, general knowledge, and love of reading.

The four levels of DK READERS are aimed at different reading abilities, enabling you to choose the books that are exactly right for each child:

Level 1 – Beginning to read
Level 2 – Beginning to read alone
Level 3 – Reading alone
Level 4 – Proficient readers

The "normal" age at which a child begins to read can be anywhere from three to eight years old, so these levels are intended only as a general guideline.

No matter which level you select, you can be sure that you are helping children learn to read, then read to learn!

LONDON, NEW YORK, DELHI,
MUNICH, AND MELBOURNE

Project Editor Louise Pritchard
Art Editor Jill Plank

Senior Editor Linda Esposito
Senior Art Editor
Diane Thistlethwaite
Production Melanie Dowland
Picture Researcher Liz Moore
Illustrator Peter Dennis
Indexer Lynn Bresler

Reading Consultant
Cliff Moon M.Ed.

Published in Great Britain by
Dorling Kindersley Limited
80 The Strand, London WC2R 0RL

Penguin Group

4 6 8 10 9 7 5

A CIP catalogue record for this book is
available from the British Library.

ISBN 0-7513-2837-5

Colour reproduction by Colourscan, Singapore
Printed and bound in China by L Rex Printing Co., Ltd.

The publisher would like to thank the following
for their kind permission to reproduce their photographs:
c=centre; b=bottom; l=left; r=right; t=top

National Geographic Image Collection: Chris Johns 26–27b; **NOAA
Photo Library/NOAA Central Library** (www/photolib.noaa.gov/):
28t, 30; **Planet Earth Pictures:** Alex Benwell 15br, Paolo Fanciulli 7br;
Robert Harding Picture Library: 16, Sheila Beougher 18bl,
Warren Faidley/Agliolo 1br, Warren Faidley/Int'l Stock 16–17, 18tr, Jeff
Greenberg 22tr; **Tony Stone Images:** 21tr, Christoph Burki 5tr, Jerry
Kobalenko 4–5, John Lund 32, Alan R Moller 19b, Camille Tokerud 15cr;
Topham Picturepoint: 25br, J. McTyre 24.

All other images © Dorling Kindersley.
For further information see: www.dkimages.com

see our complete catalogue at

www.dk.com

DK READERS

BEGINNING
TO READ ALONE
2

Twisters!

Written by Kate Hayden

DK

A Dorling Kindersley Book

Rob was working
in his farmyard in Texas.
It was a peaceful spring day but
his dog, Barney, was unhappy.
He hid under a tractor and
would not come out.
Rob wondered if Barney was ill.

Second sense

Animals have sharper senses than we have. Many can sense changes in the weather, like just before a bad storm.

Suddenly the sky went dark.
Hailstones as big as golf balls
pelted down from the sky.
Thunder rolled and
lightning flashed.
A few moments later
there was a deathly stillness.
Somehow, Barney had known!

As Bob looked on,
huge black clouds began to spin.
They bubbled at the top
like boiling milk.
Gusts of wind blew straw around.
Just then, a finger of cloud
spiralled down from the sky.
A twister!

Rob stood rooted to the spot.

The twister touched the ground.

Mud and grass swirled up

like smoke from a bonfire.

That was only the start of it.

The twister began to move.

It skipped and bounced

across the fields.

It grew bigger, faster and dirtier

as it picked up mud

from the ground.

Waterspouts

Twisters out at sea
are called waterspouts.
They whisk up water.
The tallest one seen
was 1.6 kilometres tall.

Rob watched in horror
as the twister went
towards his neighbour's farm.
It picked up straw, trees –
and even a farm truck.
It spun them around in its funnel.
Rob sighed with relief when
the twister moved away.
He thought he was safe.
But then the twister
changed direction –
straight towards him!

Suddenly the twister was hanging

right over Rob's farm.

There was a noise

like a rushing waterfall,

then – BANG!

The barn exploded

as if a bomb had gone off inside it.

Rob ran with Barney
to the cellar in his house.
His ears were hurting and
he could hardly breathe.
That's because the air pressure
inside a twister is very low.
This makes people's ears ache and
causes buildings to explode.

 Just as Rob reached
the cellar,
his front porch flew off
with an ear-splitting CRASH!
Then came a SMASH
as the house windows blew in.
Two minutes later, all was silent.

Rob came up from the cellar.
Furniture lay smashed on the floor.
Most of the doors and
windows were gone.
Rob felt lucky
to be alive.

Friends helped Rob to clean up.
They lived nearby but
their house wasn't touched.

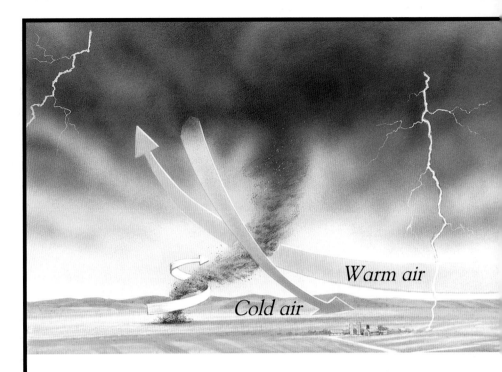

Warm air

Cold air

Twisters can form
when cold air meets warm air.
The warm air is sucked up
in a swirling column
called a funnel cloud.
It spins at great speed.
Twisters contain
the most deadly winds
in the world.

No-one knows
what a twister will do next.
It can lift up a large truck and
smash it to pieces, but
leave small objects undamaged.

One twister picked up a baby and
set him down safely
90 metres away.
The baby did not
even wake up!

Strange showers
When twisters drop
things they've picked up,
strange things can happen.
A twister in England
caused a shower of frogs.

There are lots of
strange stories
about twisters.
A twister once
blew away
a man's
birth certificate.
The twister carried it
80 kilometres
then dropped it
in a friend's garden.
One twister sucked up
some roses and water from a vase.
It dropped them
in another room but
it left the vase on the table.

Another twister picked up
a jar of pickles and carried
the jar for miles
without damaging it.

Twisters come in many different shapes and sizes. They can be thin, white and wispy. Or they can be big, thick and black.

They can even be red or green! If a twister travels across a muddy field, the mud turns it brown – and very smelly!

Twisters can grow bigger and faster
as they go along.
Some look as if they have
a loop or knot in the middle.
Some are wider at the bottom
than at the top.
Some are shaped like a tube and
others look like a slice of pie.

Lots of people
have seen a twister
from the outside.
But only a few have looked
inside a twister and survived.

A farmer named Will Keller
once looked up into a twister
from his underground shelter.
Just as he closed
the door of his shelter,
he saw lots of mini twisters
inside the big twister.
These mini twisters can rip
through a building and
slice it to shreds.

Twister speeds

Some twisters travel
only as fast as
a person walking.
Others travel
as fast as express trains.

21

Home sweet home
People stay in Tornado Alley
because it is their home.
If their houses
are destroyed,
they just rebuild.

Twisters are
also known
as tornados.
There is an area
in the USA
that is called
Tornado Alley.
It is famous for
its deadly twisters.
Up to 300 occur there
every year between April and July.
They kill more than 80 people.

Twisters form during these months
as warm air from the south meets
cold air from the north –
right over Tornado Alley.

TORNADO ALLEY

NEBRASKA

IOWA

KANSAS

MISSOURI

OKLAHOMA

ARKANSAS

TEXAS

Twisters are graded from 0 to 5
on a scale called the Fujita Scale.
An F0 damages chimneys.
An F1 snaps telephone poles.
An F2 rips off roofs.
An F3 turns over trains.
An F4 destroys even strong homes.
An F5 leaves few things standing.
In 1999, an F5 ripped through
Oklahoma City, Oklahoma.
It killed 45 people.

The worst twister
In 1925, one twister
in Tornado Alley
destroyed four towns
in less than four hours.
It killed 689 people.

People in Tornado Alley are
well prepared for twisters.
Most of them have
an underground shelter
outside their home.

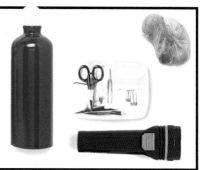

Some people in Texas have
a fibreglass shelter
buried in their back garden.

People without
a shelter hide
in a cellar
or small room
in the middle
of their house.

*The Malone family
next to their
fibreglass shelter
before it is buried*

Gary England is
a TV weather reporter
in Oklahoma City.
When lots of twisters
are expected,
Gary's team stays on the air
for 30 hours or more.

Scientists tell Gary what
the weather will be like.
Gary can then tell viewers.
The scientists use a computer
to help them forecast twisters.
The computer makes a picture
that shows where a twister is
and how fast it is travelling.

Forecasts from space
Spacecraft called satellites
orbit around Earth.
Some send information
about the weather
to scientists on Earth.

The scientists can tell Gary
what they think will happen.
But storm trackers on the road
know what is actually happening.
These people risk their lives
to find and follow twisters.
Many of them have
modern equipment
such as a satellite dish.

The trackers tell Gary
all about a twister –
where it is and
where it is going.
They can even tell him
when a twister is brewing.

In the past, people did not know when a twister was coming. Today, the trackers and scientists give people time to find shelter, and hundreds of lives are saved.

A storm tracker's modern truck

Twister facts

People in Tornado Alley
can check for twisters
when they fill their cars
with petrol.
Many pumps show
the weather forecast
on a screen.

Winds inside a twister
can spin around
at nearly
500 kilometres per hour.

In April 1974,
148 tornados tore through
13 states in the USA.
Six of them were F5s –
the strongest type of tornado.

In 1994, in Australia,
hundreds of fish fell
from the sky.
This was probably
the work of a twister.

Twisters that suck up
sand in deserts
are called dust devils.

A twister can last
for any length of time –
from a few minutes
to an hour.